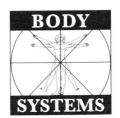

BODY SYSTEMS

Breathing

Jackie Hardie

First published in Great Britain by Heinemann Library
Halley Court, Jordan Hill, Oxford OX2 8EJ
a division of Reed Educational and Professional Publishing Ltd.

OXFORD FLORENCE PRAGUE MADRID ATHENS MELBOURNE
AUCKLAND KUALA LUMPUR SINGAPORE TOKYO IBADAN
NAIROBI KAMPALA JOHANNESBURG GABORONE
PORTSMOUTH NH (USA) CHICAGO MEXICO CITY SAO PAULO

Designed by Inklines and Small House Design
Illustrations by Catherine Ward, except: Peter Bull Art Studio, p.4 (left) &
pp 22–23; Garden Studio/Darren Patterson, p.27.

Printed in Great Britain by Bath Press Colourbooks, Glasgow
Originated in Great Britain by Dot Gradations, Wickford

01 00 99 98 97
10 9 8 7 6 5 4 3 2 1

ISBN 0 431 06213 7
This title is also available in a hardback library edition (ISBN 0 431 06212 9).

British Library Cataloguing in Publication Data
Hardie, Jackie, 1944–
    Breathing. – (Body systems)
    1. Respiration – Juvenile literature
    I. Title
    612.2

Acknowledgements
The Publishers would like to thank the following for permission to reproduce
photographs:
The Advertising Archives: p.19; Allsport: p.23; Oxford Scientific Films: p.5,
p.15, p.21 (left); Science Photo Library: p.4, p.6, p.9, p.10, p.18 (both), p.21
(right), p.29; SHOUT: p.28; Sipa Press: p.27; Telegraph Colour Library: p.17
(bottom); Tony Stone Images: p.16, p.17 (top), p.22.

Commissioned photographs p.14 & p.31: Trevor Clifford.
Cover photograph: Trevor Clifford.

Our thanks to Yvonne Hewson and Dr Kath Hadfield for their comments in
the preparation of this book.

Contents

Why you need to breathe

Most of us take for granted our bodies and the way they work. You digest the food you eat and your heart beats regularly, keeping you going. All the time you breathe air in and out without even thinking about it. You start to breathe the moment you are born. But why do you do it? To get vital **oxygen** from the air and get rid of unwanted **carbon dioxide**.

Giving you energy

If you are to stay alive, your body **cells** need energy. Your cells release energy from food by a process known as **respiration**. For this to happen, oxygen is needed.

You get the oxygen from the air around you when you breathe in. In respiration, carbon dioxide and water are made by your cells. You get rid of them when you breathe out.

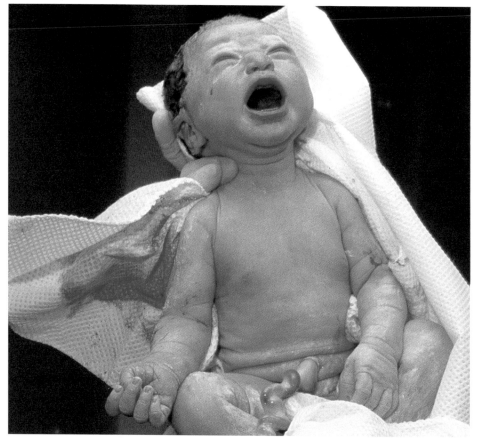

◀ A baby takes her first breath. Before she was born the baby received the oxygen she needed from her mother's blood.

Breathing surfaces

In small, thin animals, such as the flatworm, all the body cells are near the surface. Oxygen and other useful substances can move easily (but slowly) from one part of the body to another, and into and out of the body. So, many small animals can exchange gases through their body surface. But in bigger animals, special systems are needed to move things around.

A **breathing system** takes air rich in oxygen into the body to a **breathing organ**. It also takes air rich in carbon dioxide away from there. The breathing organ has a large surface packed into a small space. The top layer of the surface is very thin and is usually kept moist. Large animals have breathing organs such as lungs (in humans and other land dwellers) or gills (in fish).

▲ This water beetle breathes under water from a bubble of air it has collected.

Your breathing system

Your **breathing system** begins in your nose (and mouth) and finishes in your lungs. Air enters the system through your nose or mouth and goes into the **windpipe**. This divides into smaller and smaller tubes in your lungs. **Oxygen** in this air passes through the thin lining of the lungs and into your blood. **Red blood cells** in the blood stream then carry oxygen to the **cells** in your body. Meanwhile, the rest of the air is breathed out, along with unwanted **carbon dioxide** and **water vapour**.

Taking a deep breath

Your lungs are in your chest. This is separated from your lower body by the **diaphragm**. You can see your chest moving gently when you are breathing. This is because your brain is telling some muscles to move.

The muscles that move are between your ribs and around the diaphragm. These movements squash your lungs, so you breathe out, then the movements pull out the lungs, so you breathe in.

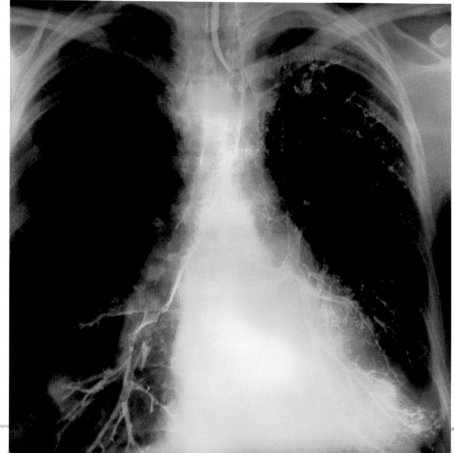

► X-ray photograph of a person's chest, showing the windpipe dividing into two tubes (the **bronchi**) and then into smaller and smaller tubes (**bronchioles**) inside the lung on the left.

Taking oxygen to your cells

Blood collects waste carbon dioxide from the cells in your body, and takes it to the lungs. Here the unwanted gas is breathed out. Blood then collects oxygen which has been breathed in.

The blood carries the oxygen to the cells. The cells use it to burn food to create energy. Carbon dioxide is made when the energy is used, and the cycle starts again.

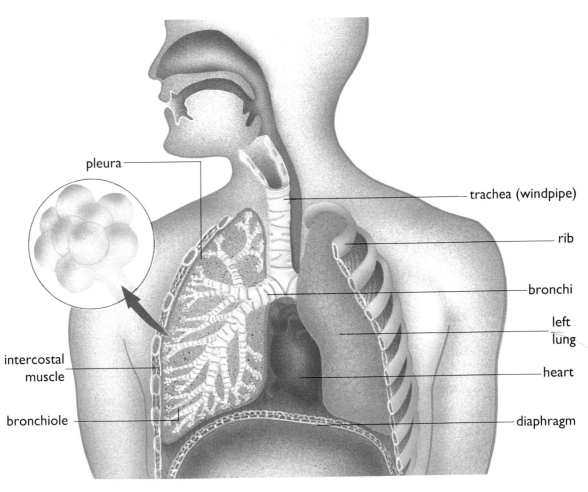

pleura

trachea (windpipe)

rib

bronchi

left lung

heart

diaphragm

intercostal muscle

bronchiole

▲ *The breathing system, from the mouth and nose to the two lungs inside the chest.*

Did you know?

Breathing usually runs on 'automatic pilot' – you don't think about it. This is just as well when you are sleeping! You can however control your breathing up to a point, which is useful for activities like swimming.

Inside your head

When you breathe in air through your nostrils, your nose does a most useful job. It warms the incoming air, filters out the dust and helps deal with the germs that are drawn in with every breath.

Inside your nose

Your nose has two nostrils. Each nostril leads into a space (a **nasal cavity**) which forms an airway that leads to your throat and then to your **windpipe** or **trachea**. The lining of the nostril is covered with a layer of **cells** that are well supplied with blood. Some of the cells in the lining make a slimy fluid called **mucus**. These cells have fine hairs, called **cilia**, which beat all the time.

These movements push a layer of mucus along, carrying dirt and dust with it. The mucus is pushed towards the nostrils, where you get rid of it when you blow your nose or sneeze. Cilia in the breathing tubes in your chest push the mucus towards the top of the windpipe and you then swallow it. If there are any germs in the mucus, they will be killed by the acid in your stomach.

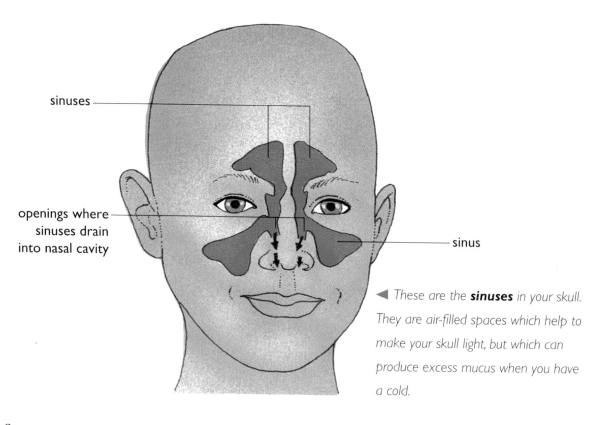

sinuses

openings where sinuses drain into nasal cavity

sinus

◄ These are the **sinuses** in your skull. They are air-filled spaces which help to make your skull light, but which can produce excess mucus when you have a cold.

Having a cold

Near the nasal cavities there are air-filled spaces called sinuses in the bones of your skull. These make your skull hollow and light. If your skull was made of solid bone it would be harder work for you to hold your head up! When you have a cold, the lining of these cavities may swell and make a lot of mucus. This may give you a runny nose or headache.

Swallowing

When you swallow, the **soft palate** blocks the airway from the nasal cavity. A small flap (the epiglottis) covers the opening of the windpipe. This means food will go down the oesophagus (food pipe) to the stomach, and not go the wrong way into the windpipe. If food lands on the epiglottis, you will cough and splutter until it goes down the right way.

► When your mouth is wide open you can see the **uvula** hanging down above the throat.

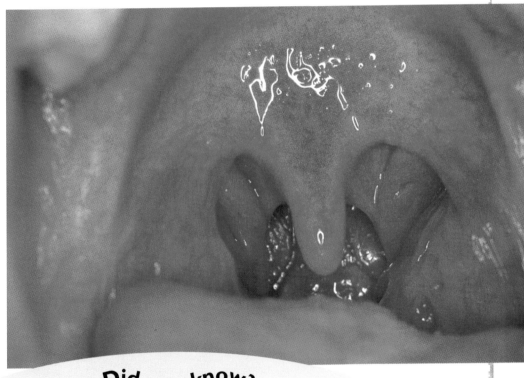

Did you know?

No one knows for sure what the the uvula at the back of your mouth is for. It is part of the soft palate and it may be there to make sure there is a good seal as the air passages are shut off when you swallow. One thing is known for sure: the uvula has nothing to do with the voice. So when you see cartoon characters with a flap that is wobbling in a frenzy, the cartoonist has got it wrong!

Inside your chest

During breathing, a lot of different things happen inside your chest. The lungs are protected by a cage made from your ribs, backbone and chest bone (sternum). This **rib cage** moves in and out as the muscles between your ribs pull on it. Other muscles attached to your **diaphragm** move it up and down. These movements either stretch your lungs and fill them with air, or squash them and squeeze the air out.

Into your lungs

When you breathe in, the air goes down the **windpipe** or **trachea**. This tube divides into two tubes called **bronchi**. Each bronchus goes into one of your lungs, then divides many times to form breathing tubes that become narrower and narrower.

These tubes are the **bronchioles**. The walls of the larger breathing tubes are strengthened by rings of **cartilage** which hold them open and allow the air to flow through freely, just like the ridges on the hose of a vacuum cleaner.

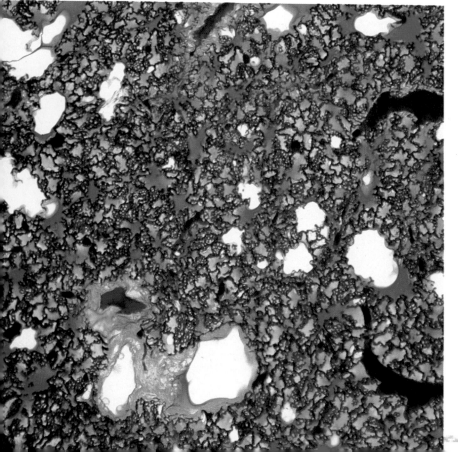

◄ If all the **air sacs** (**alveoli**) in a person's lungs could be laid flat, the total surface area for breathing would be the size of a tennis court.

Into your blood

At the tips of the finest bronchioles are the air sacs or alveoli. They look like tiny clusters of balloons, or grapes on a vine. The walls of each alveolus are very thin because the wall is only two **cells** thick. Each alveolus has a lot of very fine blood vessels (**capillaries**) around it. This means that gases can move quickly and easily from inside the alveolus through its walls into the blood in the blood vessels, and from the blood back into the alveolus.

There are about 300 million tiny air sacs filling your two lungs. If you could open the air sacs and lay them flat, they would make a carpet about 12 m long and 8 m wide, which is about the size of a tennis court. Together, these sacs, the tubes and the blood vessels make up the spongy lungs.

blood from network of capillaries

blood to network of capillaries

thin wall of the alveoli

▲ Air sacs or alveoli, with their blood supply, at the tip of a bronchiole. There are about 300 million of these in your lungs.

Did you know?

When you breathe in and out, the air you breathe moves at about 8 km per hour. But when you sneeze, the air speed is more like 160 km per hour! A single sneeze can shoot 20,000 drops of moisture into the air up to about 4 m away. So, if you have a cold, use a handkerchief to avoid infecting other people.

Breathing movements

When sitting still, you breathe about 15 to 18 times a minute. You can change how quickly or how deeply you breathe for a short time, but as soon as you stop thinking about it, your breathing goes back to normal. Each breath is about 500 cubic cm of air (about as much air as milk in a small carton). If you run, you take deeper breaths and more of them. This means more **oxygen** goes into your blood to help produce the extra energy you need.

Moving your chest

When you breathe, your chest works like a bellows and it changes shape. These changes are brought about by muscles moving your ribs and **diaphragm**. When you **inhale**, or breathe in, the diaphragm is pulled down and your **rib cage** moves up.

This makes the space inside your chest bigger. Air rushes in to fill the space. In **exhaling**, or breathing out, the diaphragm moves up and the rib cage is lowered. The space inside your chest gets smaller and you breathe out. Air is forced out of the lungs.

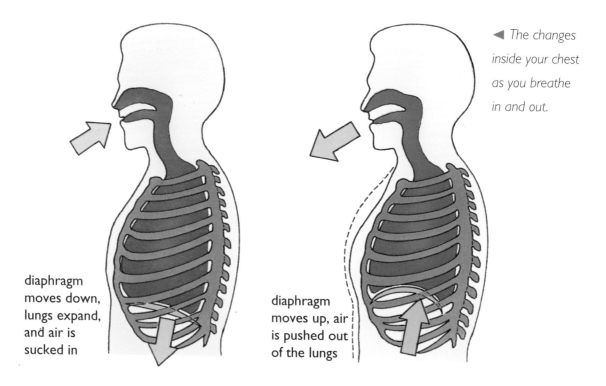

◀ *The changes inside your chest as you breathe in and out.*

diaphragm moves down, lungs expand, and air is sucked in

diaphragm moves up, air is pushed out of the lungs

Pleural layers

The lungs are surrounded by a tough double layer, the **pleura**. In the space between the layers there is a fluid which is slippery. The outer pleura lines the rib cage and diaphragm.

The inner one forms a layer on the lungs. These pleural layers and the fluid between them help to make breathing movements smooth and stop the ribs damaging the lungs.

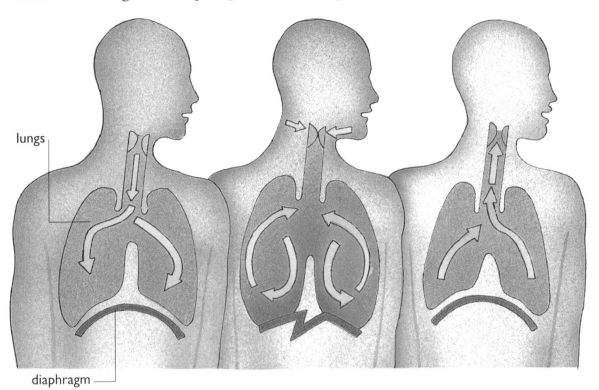

lungs

diaphragm

normal breath in

diaphragm twitches, top of breathing tubes snap shut

normal breath out

▲ Twitch of the diaphragm during hiccups.

Hiccups

If you get hiccups, the diaphragm is twitching (or in rhythmic spasm). Surprisingly, eating too much can give you hiccups. So can eating spicy foods, or swallowing foods which are too hot or too cold. There are many cures and you have to find one that works for you. Some people breathe the same air in from and out into a paper bag. Others hold their breath!

Did you know?

When you get a stitch, you have cramp in your diaphragm. If you bend over and touch your toes, the diaphragm is usually stretched enough to relieve the cramp.

What happens to the air you breathe?

Air is a mixture of gases including **oxygen**, **nitrogen** and a small amount of **water vapour** and **carbon dioxide**. Air that is breathed in and air that is breathed out contain different amounts of gases. Breathing removes some oxygen and adds carbon dioxide and water vapour. If you breathe out onto a cold window or mirror, the water vapour you breathe out will condense and change into liquid water, making the glass 'steam up'.

Respiration and energy

Respiration is a process that goes on in every living **cell**. Sugar from the food you eat is burnt up, using oxygen. This releases energy which keeps your body working. The sugar and oxygen are used up inside the cells. Two waste substances are made, carbon dioxide and water vapour. Some of the water may be used by the cells but some will be breathed out with the carbon dioxide. The chemical changes that happen in respiration mean that **exhaled** air is different to the air you breathe in.

◀ The water vapour in the air you breathe out will condense, or change into liquid, on cool surfaces.

Moving gases around the body

Respiration uses oxygen and makes carbon dioxide. These gases are moved around the body by the blood. **Red blood cells** carry the oxygen and this **oxygenated blood** is bright red. The red blood cells then pass close to the cells which need oxygen.

The oxygen leaves the blood and carbon dioxide enters it. The resulting **de-oxygenated blood** is a dull red. Back in the lungs, the carbon dioxide passes from the blood and into the **air sacs** or **alveoli**, and it is then breathed out.

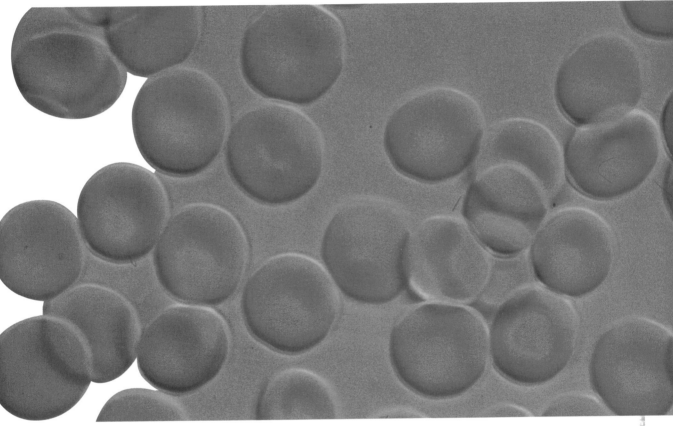

▲ Red blood cells.

Did you know?

Tourists have been banned from visiting some sites where there are prehistoric cave paintings. They have also been stopped from visiting the inside of some of the pyramids in Egypt. This is because over the years the breathed-out air of many tourists – and the carbon dioxide it contains – has damaged the paintings or the stone.

Pollution

Our **breathing system** works best when the air is clean. But today, the air often contains harmful gases, such as **sulphur dioxide** and **carbon monoxide**, as well as **oxygen**. These gases come mainly from factories and other industrial sites, from motor cars, and from cigarette smoke. The damage such waste products cause to our natural and everyday surroundings is called **pollution**.

Air pollution

Burning fossil fuels, such as coal, oil and natural gas, produces sulphur dioxide and carbon monoxide. Sulphur dioxide dissolves in rainwater and may be carried away from the place it was made. When sulphur dioxide dissolves in water it forms an acid, so when the gas is breathed in it may irritate the moist linings of breathing passages and cause a runny nose. The breathing tubes and **air sacs** in the lungs may be damaged by this acid, too, and this makes lung diseases more likely.

◄ *Smoke from factory chimneys can cause damage to health.*

Car exhausts

Burning fuels, such as petrol, produces carbon monoxide. If this gas reaches a **red blood cell**, it will stop the cell carrying oxygen. So, to carry oxygen the body will need to make new red cells. If there is a lot of carbon monoxide, people will have to breathe faster to get the oxygen they need.

▲ The fumes in car exhausts may contain many dangerous chemicals, like carbon monoxide, ozone, unburned hydrocarbons, lead and oxides of nitrogen.

The smoke from car exhausts may also contain lead. This is from tetraethyl lead, which is added to petrol so the car engine runs smoothly. Today, lead-free petrol is available. New cars run on it. The lead in exhaust from cars can be removed by attaching a **catalytic converter** to the engine. In the 1980s, it was found that children living near motorways had high levels of lead in their blood. This may interfere with the development of their brains.

Did you know?

Many industries produce chemicals that pollute the air. This may damage the lungs of workers in the industry and of people who live nearby. Miners are likely to suffer from a disease called pneumoconiosis. Workers in asbestos factories may suffer from asbestosis. In this the fibres from asbestos become embedded in the lungs.

▲ This worker is wearing a mask, which cleans the air he is breathing.

Smoking

Cigarettes are made from the dried, shredded leaves of the tobacco plant. The habit of **inhaling** smoke for pleasure started hundreds of years ago, probably in South America. The smoke from burning tobacco contains dozens of chemicals. The main drug in cigarette smoking is nicotine. It is likely to be **addictive**, making it harder for the smoker to give up the habit of smoking.

Damage from nicotine

Nicotine and **tar** breathed in with cigarette smoke may stop the cleaning **cells** in the breathing tubes from working. Nicotine also enters the blood through the lungs and affects the nervous system. Tar collects deep in the lungs and stains them brown. This may lead to serious illness, such as cancer of the lung. Smokers are more likely than non-smokers to have serious diseases.

People who smoke die, on average, at a younger age than people who don't smoke. For instance, a 25-year-old man who smokes 40 cigarettes a day can expect to live 8.3 years fewer than one who does not. You don't even have to light up yourself. If you are with smokers, you breathe in the smoke from their cigarettes. This **passive smoking** can seriously damage your health.

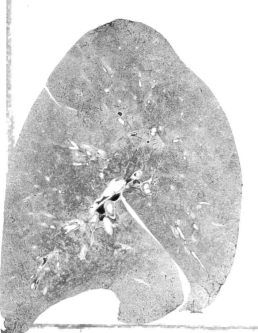

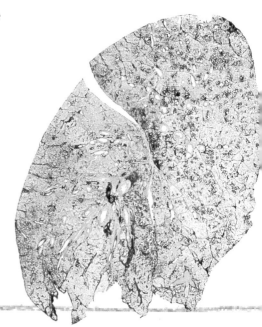

◄ ► *Tar deposits in one of these sections (thin slices) of two human lungs show clearly which lung belonged to a smoker and which to a non-smoker.*

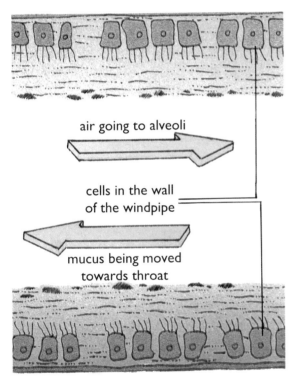

▲ *In the windpipe, dust and dirt are trapped in sticky mucus. The **cilia** beat to move the dirty mucus away from the lungs.*

air going to alveoli

cells in the wall of the windpipe

mucus being moved towards throat

Did you know?
About 100,000 people in the UK die each year as a direct result of smoking.

▲ *Governments in many countries advertise the dangers of smoking with posters like this one.*

Breathlessness

Smokers get out of breath easily. They also produce a lot of **mucus** and they have to cough to remove it. This can lead to **bronchitis**. **Carbon monoxide** from smoke gets into the **red blood cells** and stops them from carrying **oxygen**. So a smoker may have to breathe faster and this can strain the heart.

Pregnancy

Many substances in the mother's blood pass into her baby's blood in her **womb**. This includes drugs such as alcohol and the chemicals from cigarette smoke. Pregnant women who smoke are more likely to lose the baby before it is fully developed (have a miscarriage). They are also more likely to have a baby who dies in the first week after birth.

Asthma

In the western world, about 3 people out of 100 suffer from **asthma**. Asthma is more common in people who live in the cities than among those who live in the countryside. Sometimes asthma is triggered by **allergens** in the surroundings, like car exhaust fumes, **house dust mites** or **pollen** grains. For some people, even laughing, frying food or the smell of paint may start an asthma attack.

What is asthma?

'Asthma' means 'to breathe hard'. If you have asthma you may get sudden attacks of shortness of breath and wheezing, especially when you breathe out. Your chest feels tight and you often get a cough. The attack passes and breathing returns to normal.

During an attack, three things happen in your lungs at the same time. The muscles in the walls of the breathing tubes contract, more **mucus** is made there, and the inside walls of the tubes swell. If treated quickly all three things can be put back to normal.

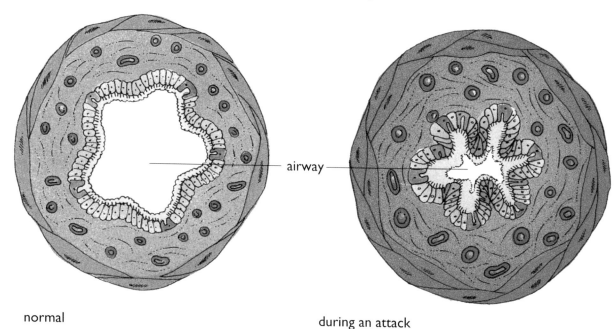

normal   during an attack

▲ *This is what happens during an asthma attack. A slice through a **bronchiole** shows how the airway becomes narrow and makes breathing difficult.*

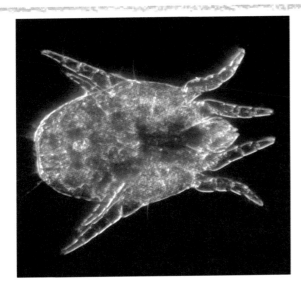

▲ *A house dust mite, much magnified. Many people believe mites in carpets, mattresses and household dust trigger asthma attacks.*

Treating asthma

During an attack, an asthma sufferer may need an **inhaler**. This contains a drug which opens up (dilates) the breathing tubes, so the drug is known as a broncho-dilator. If you use an inhaler it is important to take in a deep breath at the same time as you press down the top of the inhaler. This helps to get the spray of the drug into the lungs where it is needed.

▲ *This girl is using an inhaler to spray a broncho-dilator drug into her lungs. This helps to widen the breathing tubes.*

Did you know?

Many people have asthma. But with the right treatment it should not spoil their lives. Famous athletes who have been successful despite having asthma include the British runner Sebastian Coe, cricketer Ian Botham, water skier Liz Hobbs, and the American Olympic sprint champion, Florence Griffiths-Joyner.

Breathing in unusual places

Astronauts and deep-sea divers work where there is no air. They must be given a special supply of air to stay alive. Usually, the air is supplied from cylinders.

Breathing under water

The first aqualung or scuba (self contained underwater breathing apparatus) was invented by the Frenchman, Jacques Cousteau, in 1942. When a diver works at a great depth, the water presses heavily on the chest. This makes it harder to breathe, so to help the diver, air is supplied at high pressure in a scuba which is carried on the back.

At these high pressures the **nitrogen** in the air dissolves in the blood, as well as the **oxygen**. This doesn't matter while the diver is deep down. But if he or she comes up quickly, the nitrogen comes out of the blood as air bubbles. It hurts to bend the limbs and the diver has 'the bends'. The diver will die if bubbles form in the fine blood vessels of the brain and heart.

◀ *People working under water need a supply of air. They wear aqualungs.*

Breathing in high places

In the high mountains, the amount of oxygen in the air is less than at sea level. When people arrive by air at cities in high places they find it hard to breathe. They may get out of breath even when sleeping. However, they get used to the air if they live in such a place for a week or two. This is called getting acclimatized. Their bodies have made more **red blood cells**. Their blood can carry more oxygen, enough to supply all the **cells** of the body.

Did you know?

If you could count the number of red blood cells in 1 cubic millimetre (1mm³) of blood (about as much as would be in this spot:•), you would find 5,000,000. Five million! People who live all their lives at high altitude have over 7 million!

Some athletes train at high altitude, to make more red blood cells, so the blood can carry more oxygen. When the athletes return to places nearer sea level, they may be able to perform better in their event than athletes who have not trained in this way. Champion distance runners from countries such as Kenya and Ethiopia may owe some of their success to the fact that they grew up in places high above sea level.

◄ Moses Kiptanui of Kenya wins the steeplechase at the 1995 World Championships in Gothenburg, Sweden.

Your voice

When you speak, the sounds you make come from the **voicebox**, or **larynx**, at the top of the **windpipe**. Sounds are made when air passes over your **vocal cords**. Sounds are shaped into recognizable words by your lips, teeth and tongue.

In the voice box

You can feel your voice box, or larynx, at the front of your neck. It is at the top end of the windpipe, or **trachea**. The sides of the larynx are kept rigid by **cartilage**. The inner lining of the voice box has two pairs of folds. The upper pair forms a valve that allows you to hold your breath under water.

The lower pair, the vocal cords, stretch across the opening from the front to the back. The vocal cords are two flat, white bands. They are about 13–18 mm long in women, 17–25 mm long in men. Most of the time your vocal cords are kept apart. Air flows freely through the V-shaped opening between them and no sound is made.

▶ The voice box is at the top of the windpipe and it contains the vocal cords.

windpipe

voice box cartilage

oesophagus (food pipe)

Making the sounds

When the vocal cords are stretched and air from your lungs is forced between them, the cords tremble, or vibrate, and a sound is made. If the vocal cords are stretched tight and close together, the sound is high-**pitched**: the cords vibrate many times in a short period.

When the vocal cords are looser and further apart, the sound is low-pitched. The range of a particular person's voice – the difference between the high and low-pitched sounds that the voice produces – depends on the thickness and length of their vocal cords.

▲ This girl can feel her vocal cords when she says something.

Did you know?

The number of vibrations of the vocal cords ranges from about 80 per second in a man talking in a deep voice, to about 1400 per second in a woman singing in a very high-pitched tone. The number of vibrations is called the frequency.

Turning sounds into words

Most mammals – humans, dogs, cattle, mice, and so on – have a **voice box**. But only humans produce the great variety of sounds known as **speech**. People combine sounds in different ways, to form the words of a **language**.

Forming words

When you speak, air passes between the **vocal cords** and goes on up to the space behind your tongue, into your mouth, and between the lips. Movements of your lips, and of the tongue against the roof of the mouth (the **palate**) and teeth, shape the sound into words.

Most of the words you speak are a combination of vowels (sounds like 'oh', 'ah', 'eeh') and consonants (sounds like 'tee' and 'dee'). When you make an 'f' sound, your top teeth are over your lower lip as you force air through. If you put your tongue under your top teeth and blow through your lips you will get a 'th' sound. In an 'm' or an 'n' sound, the air in the **nasal cavity** vibrates.

Intonation

In some languages, the meaning of the rise and fall in the **pitch** of the voice is spread over a whole sentence. In other languages, called tonal languages (Chinese, or Cantonese, is one example), **intonation** is used to distinguish single words. So the same combination of sounds making a word can have three meanings depending on whether it is said with a rising, falling, or level tone.

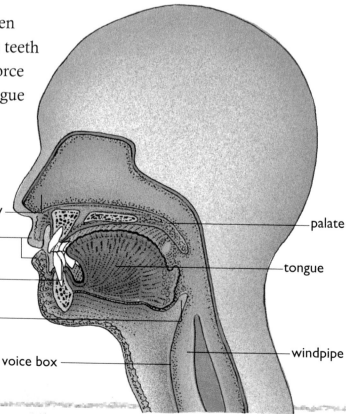

nasal cavity

lips

teeth

epiglottis

palate

tongue

windpipe

voice box

▶ Parts of the mouth that are important in producing speech.

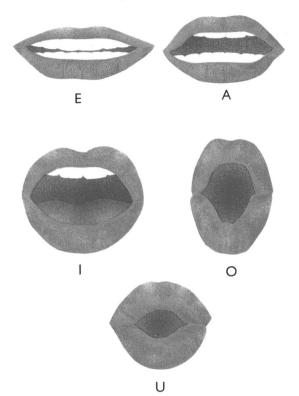

E   A

I   O

U

▲ *The lips form a different shape for each*
vowel sound.

Did you know?

The Khoisan languages of southern Africa use clicks and other types of 'stop' made in the throat or nose. One such language has 48 different click sounds.

Unfamiliar sounds

Some speech sounds do not use the air stream from the lungs. One of the most common is the 'click', a sharp sound made by the tongue or lips. You probably use a click sound to show disapproval. In some languages, in southern Africa for example, clicks are used as consonants. So even though clicks are very common, these languages may sound strange to people who are unfamiliar with this use of clicks.

► *Singer Miriam Makeba uses click sounds*
in the songs she sings from southern Africa.

Artificial breathing

Some accidents cause a person to stop breathing. This is called **asphyxia**. It may happen when someone drowns or has an **epileptic fit**. It is important to help to get **oxygen** into the casualty's blood. More than four minutes without oxygen could cause serious brain damage. If you know what to do in these situations, it could save somebody's life.

Artificial resuscitation

Starting the breathing again is called artificial resuscitation. All emergency workers are trained to do it. The worker checks that the mouth and throat are clear. Then they breathe out air into the casualty's mouth or nose. This air contains oxygen.

If they blow into the mouth, the casualty's nose must be held closed, but if blowing into the nose, the mouth must be closed. Either way, it is important to tilt the casualty's head well back, so that the tongue does not flop over the **windpipe**.

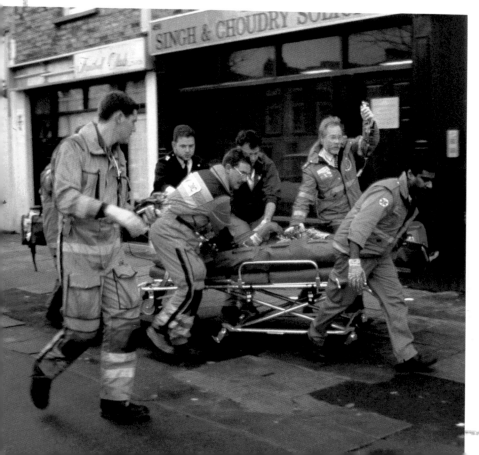

◄ Doctors, emergency workers and paramedics who attend accidents are all trained to do artificial resuscitation.

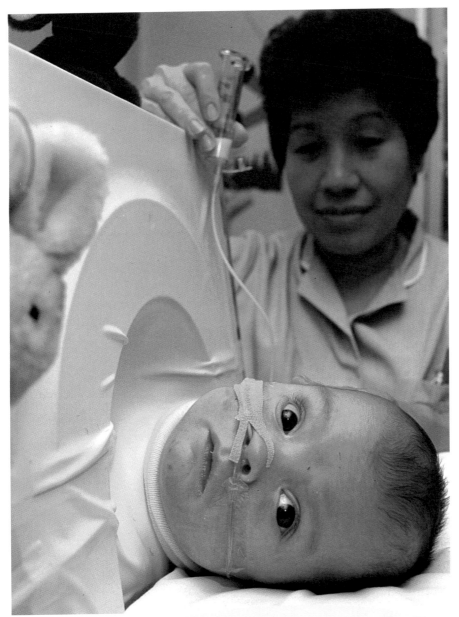

◄ The little boy has paralyzed breathing muscles . An iron lung machine helps him to breathe.

Did you know?

Some diseases, such as polio, may stop the muscles used for breathing from working. This means the person with the disease could die from asphyxia. The first life-saving iron lung was designed in 1929. In an iron lung, a pump creates a vacuum in an airtight box that encloses the patient's chest. The pump works in such a way that the vacuum is on and then off. Each time the vacuum is on, the pressure of the air is greater outside the box than inside it and inside the patient's chest. So air is sucked into the patient's chest.

Glossary

Addictive Makes you crave for more, or want more.

Air sacs Thin-walled endings to the breathing tubes. This is where oxygen from the air you breathe in is transferred into your blood.

Allergens Substances that produce a reaction in the body and prevent it working properly.

Alveoli See **Air sacs**.

Asphyxia Being unable to breathe.

Asthma Condition that affects the breathing tubes and makes it hard to breathe.

Breathing organ The structure in animals where oxygen passes into the blood.

Breathing system The tubes and structures in the body that allow you to breathe.

Bronchi Two tubes which branch from the windpipe and lead to the lungs.

Bronchioles Fine tubes inside the lungs that transport air to the air sacs.

Bronchitis Disease of the bronchi and bronchioles.

Capillary Very fine blood vessel.

Carbon dioxide One of the gases in the air. It is also the waste gas given off by cells when they use oxygen to burn food to release energy. Blood collects it from the cells, carries it to the lungs, and it is breathed out.

Carbon monoxide A gas found in car exhaust fumes.

Cartilage Firm smooth substance.

Catalytic converter Device fitted to car exhausts, which reduces the amount of dangerous gases in exhaust fumes.

Cells The tiny 'building blocks' of living things.

Cilia Tiny hairs on the surface of cells. The hairs beat in a rhythmical way.

De-oxygenated blood Dull red blood that is poor in oxygen, rich in carbon dioxide.

Diaphragm The sheet of tissue in your body that separates the chest from the lower body.

Epileptic fit A fit which people who suffer from epilepsy, a nervous disease, may have.

Exhale Breathe out.

House dust mite Tiny spider-like animals found in house dust. They are too small for you to see them.

Inhale Breathe in.

Inhaler A device used by asthma sufferers to spray helpful drugs into their lungs.

Intonation Changes in the pitch of a voice speaking.

Language Combination of sounds into the words that are used to communicate between people.

Larynx The part of the windpipe containing the vocal cords.

Mucus A slimy substance made by cells.

Nasal cavity The spaces in the head that are linked to the nostrils.

Nitrogen The gas that makes up 80% of the air.

Oxygen A gas in air which is used in the body to release energy from food.

Oxygenated blood Bright red blood, which is rich in oxygen.

Palate See **Soft palate.**

Passive smoking Breathing in air that contains other people's cigarette smoke.

Pitch Your voice is high or low-pitched depending on the frequency of vibration of your vocal cord.

Pleura Layers of tissue between the lungs and ribs, which help to make breathing movements smooth.

Pollen Fine powder made by flowering plants.

Pollution Damage to the surroundings caused by human activities, especially by waste products.

Red blood cells Cells in the blood which carry oxygen.

Respiration The process in living cells which releases energy from food.

Rib cage The protective structure inside your chest. It is formed by your ribs, bones which protect your heart and lungs, and which help to bring about breathing movements.

Sinuses Spaces in the bones at the front of the skull.

Soft palate Found at the back of the roof of the mouth.

Speech Sounds formed into words.

Sulphur dioxide A waste gas found in some factory smoke.

Tar A substance breathed in with cigarette smoke.

Trachea The windpipe that leads from your mouth to your chest.

Uvula The projection at the back of the soft palate.

Vocal cords Two membranes (thin sheets of tissue) stretched across the space inside the voice-box.

Voice box See **Larynx.**

Water vapour Water in gas form.

Windpipe See **Trachea.**

Womb The part of a woman's body where a fertilized egg develops into a baby.

Index